C000269224

ADVENTURES IN
THE LEA VALLEY

ADVENTURES IN
THE LEA VALLEY

Polly Braden & David Campany

HOXTON MINI PRESS

To order books, collector's editions and signed prints go to:

www.hoxtonminipress.com

East London Photo Stories

Book Twelve

INTRODUCTION

London's Lea Valley is strange, exciting, ugly, beautiful and unaccountably mysterious. It stretches down from the Chiltern Hills, near Luton, through east London, meeting the Thames opposite the Millennium Dome. Between the two, it's an unplanned patchwork of nature reserves, social housing, yuppie apartments, small industries, scrap yards, football pitches, golf courses, cycle tracks, forgotten architecture and vast areas of nothing in particular. Threading it all together is the Lea (or Lee) River, and its canal. A green and wet world, close to the city. There are Londoners who are drawn to its enigmatic allure, and Londoners who don't even know it is there.

Polly and I began taking these photographs in 2004, the year we met. Polly was working on documentary projects for magazines and newspapers. I only ever made pictures when I wasn't writing. Together we began to spend all our spare time in the Lea Valley. We explored mostly by bicycle with one camera, and one light meter between us. We followed the seasons. Polly was a portraitist of great empathy. I liked landscapes with strange incidents. We both admired the best street photography. Somehow we combined all those elements, responding to light, space, colour and chance encounters. For long days we cycled and talked, looking, staring, watching, observing. Within a few months we were making the kinds of photographs neither of us would have made alone.

The Lea Valley is photogenic, no doubt about that. But how could we get the peculiar feeling of the place into pictures? And what about the social and economic contradictions? The ecological fragility? The endearingly haphazard character of it all? We just kept shooting, knowing one day we would look back at the mountain of photographs and make some sense of it.

Through the winter and spring of 2005, the mood along the Lea began to change. Parts of its southern end were to be the site of the 2012 Olympics. There was great concern the place would be destroyed. Often we found ourselves in the fields at the proposed site for the main stadium, close to Hackney Wick and Old Ford, where the Lea braids into several waterways. There was a beautiful Victorian metal footbridge, painted light blue. Someone had daubed on it: *Fuck Seb Coe*. Community groups were mobilizing to resist the Olympic Bid. Beyond the Lea there was little belief that London would be awarded the Games but, on July 6, it was. Nationally there was excitement. In east London feelings were mixed. On July 7, in another global context entirely, London was hit by coordinated suicide bomb attacks. It was a disconcerting time. We stopped making these photographs, got married and had two girls.

The Olympic Games came and went, and the lower Lea Valley began to come to terms with the legacy. Inevitably, we were lured back to see what had happened. Instead of pragmatic wilderness there were now landscaped parks, manicured greens, and the continuous sprouting of what property developers like to call 'luxury apartments'. In the shadow of the looming stadium, the little blue bridge remains, the graffiti long erased.

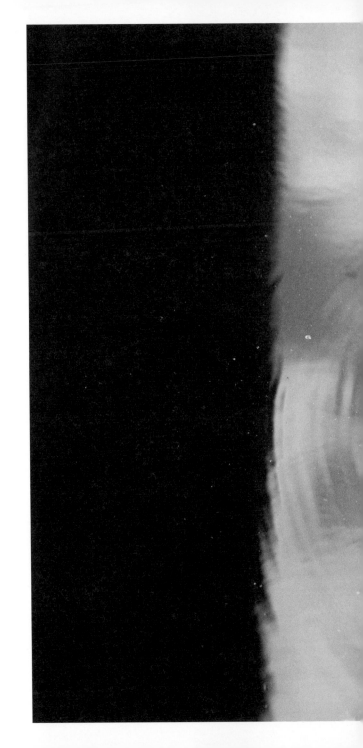

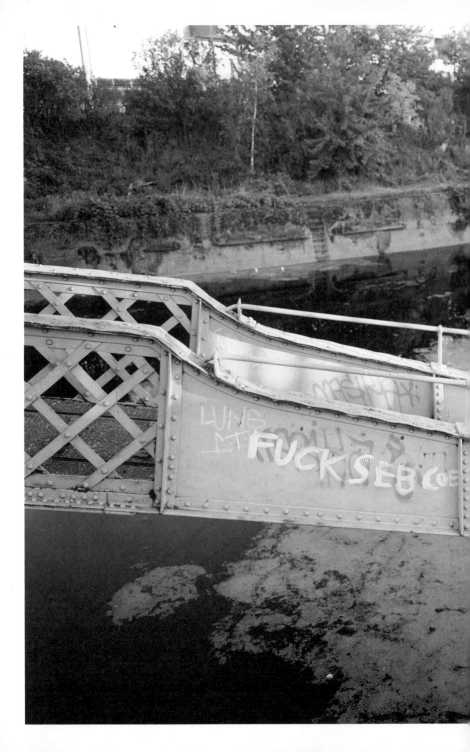

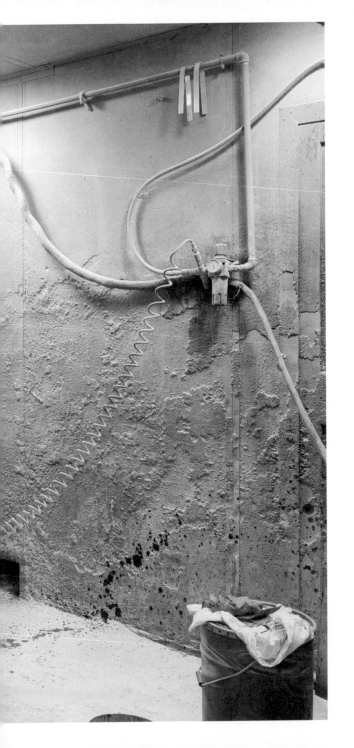

Adventures in the Lea Valley
First Edition

Copyright © Hoxton Mini Press 2016. All rights reserved.

All photographs © Polly Braden & David Campany
Intro text by David Campany
Design and sequence by Polly Braden, David Campany and Hoxton Mini Press
Series design by breadcollective.co.uk

A CIP catalogue record for this book is available from the British Library.

ISBN 978-1-910566-12-1

First published in the United Kingdom in 2016 by Hoxton Mini Press

No part of this publication may be reproduced, stored in a retrieval system, or
transmitted in any form or by any means, electronic, mechanical, photocopying,
recording or otherwise, without the prior written permission of the copyright owner.

Printed and bound by: WKT, China

To order books, collector's editions and signed prints please go to:
www.hoxtonminipress.com

MIX
Paper from
responsible sources
FSC® C010256
FSC
www.fsc.org